Mijn Reflecties, Mijn Schaduw

EMILY CARPENTER

Mijn Reflecties, Mijn Schaduw

Written by Emily Carpenter

Title by Peter-Paul de Meijer

Cover Art by Emily Timmerman

Doo Doo Style Publication

Version 1 2018

ISBN: 0-9971422-3-5
ISBN-13: 978-0-9971422-3-5

Printed and bound in the United States of America.

The following poems featured from 2016 "Hidden Messages: The Subtlety of Oppression" exhibit at Saint Louis Kranzberg Arts Center. www.kranzbergartscenter.org 1. "Ghosts of the Middle Class" 2. "Caste" 3. "The Choice" 4. What It Feels Like For a Girl" Accompanying art not included in Mijn Reflecties, Mijn Shadow. Visit www.americanfemalebook.com/art to view poetry and art exhibit in full.

For more information about permission to reproduce selections from this book, write to yodoodoostyle@gmail.com

DEDICATION

For my cousins,
Doug Knapp and Jeff Kyle,
and dear friend,
Orlanda J. Smith.

Making it a point
to say all the words I need to say
in this lifetime.

In honor of those
Who we can only feel,
and no longer hear.

CONTENTS

FOREWORD

If feel-good is what you seek,
you won't find it within these pages.

There is no balance -
only extremes -
through the darkest thoughts
and brightest days.

Leaving the strings of the four chambers
remaining with no slack.

- - -

"If you can feel what I'm feeling it's a musical masterpiece, hear
what I'm feeling, well, that's cool, at least." - Adam 'MCA' Yauch

ISOLATION
1 A

toss me aside -
i never mattered anyway -
a fun afternoon.

steal my soul
and live off of it.
while i wilt alone.

2 L

sliding down the marble cavern
disappearing into the abyss
i am swallowed by the black

my shadow stays behind
to live for me
in 2D
when i have no will

i soak in the blue hue of loneliness
and gray matter pours from my skull
it surrounds us. all. the. time.
so this is nothing new

smoke rings
forged by white hot apathy
litter the air

screaming silently
begging to return to their original form
they want to feel
so do i

broken and jagged
my nails claw
at the shiny rock

i don't make it out
yet my hands bleed
and i feel
the pain.

joyous.
i am but alive.

3 O

i allow the tears to fall
quarterly
lest they build up inside
and drown me from within

4 N

stiff heart until the blood flows

spirit transcends

i put on a show

just to feel

any love that i can -

fill the basin

overflowing. and

soak

when the drought

runs me

bone dry.

5 E

when the sun rises
all is forgotten
in a state of innocence

until

you remember.

then it is up to you
to get out of bed.

OPPRESSION
6 GHOSTS OF THE MIDDLE CLASS

middle class america
isn't aware they don't exist
blinded by their pride
and weary from their lives

they lock it all in a box. upon it

they stack scrolls of praise
defending their masters
until it can bear no more

and the box shatters

realization and resentment
pour from the remains
examining a life unlived
only through work for other's gain

don't let it be you.

7 CASTE

the weight of what i was born without
at times
smothers me

the united states of america
the land of the free

with never ending ladders to climb
as long as your plot has a tree

alas

rungs cannot be made without wood
you can plant seeds, sure
and your daughter's daughter's daughter's (son's)

maybe

have a chance
to climb and see
the majestic land of opportunity

but for now
for you
and for me

we plant seeds

and plot to scale another's pipeline to
prosperity.

8 THE CHOICE

women have choices.

two.

both are

an incomplete

existence.

9 WHAT IT FEELS LIKE FOR A GIRL

the concept of gender
manifests as medieval chains around my wrists
they've long ago rubbed them raw

the blood is dark and dry
i do not notice it anymore
it has always been my burden

forced to stand aside
a ghost of who i never became
so they can point and laugh.

fully self-actualized
as a free woman,
i am crucitfied.

i am to be a drone if i want acceptance

an effective torture device.

10 FOR MY OWN GOOD

the glass ceiling holds me down
"to keep me from falling off"

the world turns -
i know it is
to keep me dizzy

the vault locks
to keep me safe

pristine.

i pick the lock
dripping red anguish
i will not be your toy.

LOVE
11 SUNSHINE

some days the sunshine
will make you sob with memories
of when you were loved.

the feeling bounces around your heart
for a while
before settling in the pit of your gut
where all bittersweet tastes go to fade away
eventually -
hopefully.

one can only wish for the comfort of the rain
a stormy night rolling in
with the beauty of flashes of lightning
to distract you
from the pain -
and the rumbling of thunder
to drown your mourning tears.

the soil is flooded
running off the top
and beneath -
you can start again.

12 IN A BLACK ROOM

in a black room
i can be loved.

what is done in the dark -
when it is the landscape of life?

Sometimes it's almost
but always it's never.

crying sounds of my name
grasping me close in desperation

the pumpkin appears
and the light has shown

i stand alone.

13 THE LONELIEST MAN

sometimes
the black tar hollows out a cavity
in my chest.

the essence of
the unrequited
seeps from my pores.

pheromones of
the loneliest man
reappear
and cast the jesters out.

i sit upon the throne.
a tear slides down my check.

be strong.
i am obliged.

14 SOFT CLOUD OF LOVE

the soft cloud
of love
clings to me

when the time is right
i will
settle the beautiful mist
upon another

drenching us together
the heaviness of
comfort
will return

i can feel it.
i believe.

15 NEVER BEEN GOOD AT MATH

he wears the sash

not quite the crown

but i unlock the door

because i need the love in his eyes.

the runner-up gazes at his angel

as she feels the absence of Him.

the points sear through her flesh;

sacred geometry -

of lovers entangled.

as he caresses her ever-so-gently,
she cringes.

and wishes he were gone.

LESSONS
16 TIME

time
reveals our true selves
drowned beneath the surface

releases our fears
from the depths of the ocean floor

but stuck in the reef
we meander around the sea

becoming late

and in a moment
the darkness is no more

we know.

arms outstretched
fingertips grasping
for the light

alas
it is
TOO LATE

the sun has set forever

ON THAT

time

finally taught us our lesson
only for next time

17 A NOBLE QUEST

If this life

is a journey through solitude

(for only me - it be fit)

i cry mercy

waving my white flag

abandoning Pan

as i reluctantly

step back over the line

a noble quest,

it seemed, at first,

but -

ironically,

i was mistaken.

18 LET'S BE CLEAR

My transparency

is startlingly
out of place.

it is never
clear enough
to wash away.

it colors
my life
my days
my love.

the 'absence of'
has been responsible for
missing pieces of my soul
of the same name.

19 THE ARMOR

the armor
shiny many moons ago
a point of pride

has rusted in place

creaking and groaning
with every move

embedded
down to the bone

chiseled away
it dissolves in the wind

exposing raw marrow
vulnerable

to the harsh seasons of life

but behind it
one is numb

life or death

it is the only choice

20 SADNESS

sadness
is another way
to feel
you are alive

tears
sliding down your cheeks
Tell you what
you
already know

be grateful.

ABOUT THE AUTHOR

Emily is a multi-disciplinary artist and storyteller living in Brooklyn, NY with her senior chihuahua min-pin mix, Bebe. Film and painting are areas of creative interests as of late, along with the usuals: travel, sunshine, and healing.

Read AMERICAN FEMALE: a true tale of adventure to learn more about Emily. Watch the trailers at www.americanfemalebook.com

www.ingramcontent.com/pod-product-compliance
Lightning Source LLC
Chambersburg PA
CBHW021150020426
42331CB00005B/981